31 Days of Praying God's Wisdom for My Children

31 Days of Praying God's Wisdom for My Children

Moms Gathering God's Valuable Wisdom from the Book of Proverbs and persistently covering Our Precious Children in Prayer

**Verses Quoted taken from the
New Century Version**

Hope McCardy

For information, please write:

Hope McCardy
P. O. Box SS-6763
Nassau, Bahamas
info@empoweringyourhope.com
www.empoweringyourhope.com

ISBN 10: 1533305625
ISBN 13: 9781533305626 (electronic)

Printed in the United States of America.

Wisdom will come into your mind, and
knowledge will be pleasing to you.
Good sense will protect you; understanding
will guard you.
It will keep you from the wicked, from those
whose words are bad.

PROVERBS 2:10-12

To my wonderful and precious children: Kristi Collie, Rashad, Nicole, and Adria McCardy. You've taught me how to search for God's wisdom and guidance on a regular basis. I thank God that you too are learning the vast importance of prayer.

Contents

FOREWORD

For as long as I have known myself, I knew that my mother was praying for me – for my present and future. I am confident that her prayers have been the source of my success in life thus far. One example has been her continuously asking for blessings upon my relationships and, at the time, my future husband. As a result of knowing that she was praying on my behalf, even as a teenager, I was prompted to start journaling and praying for my future husband. So much so, that on our wedding day, I was able to give Wendell, my now husband, a book filled with all the things I had prayed for him. I know that I have a godly, caring, and strong man in my life because of my mommy praying for him.

I truly thank God for her and that He honored her and my prayers from years ago. This proof positive is only one of the reasons why I believe in the importance of praying for your children. And God always keeps His word as He answers our prayers! Thanks for your example, Mom.

Kristi Collie (29)

There's something about growing up with a mother who's constantly praying for her children. My mom quite often made me question whether or not my view on how I prayed to God needed to change, and time and time again it did. Growing up, I believed that I was only to pray to God when something was important or for an event that was close at hand. However, my mother, from the time we were kids would pray for our future spouses. She made me realize that God has no limit, and it's never too early or too late to pray to Him. I began praying about almost anything no matter how far it was in the future – all because I have a mother who is continuously praying for her one and only son. I love you, Mom.

Rashad McCardy (27)

"Prayer makes things happen!" This motto is definitely something that I have learned from my mother. She has literally covered every aspect of my life in prayer, both big and small. Through example, she has shown me that nothing is too little or insignificant to bring to God. My mother is the leading supporter in my life. No matter where I am, I honestly call her to tell her every little thing I have going on in my days, which she responds to with the same excitement. I could never be the person I am today without her, and I am so proud of her accomplishments.

Nicole McCardy (24)

To be honest, sometimes I don't even know how to pray, or what to pray for, but my mom certainly does. Anytime I need assistance or direction, she can always point out the scriptures that will help to guide my steps and prayers. She is always ready to join me in prayer, fasting, or even goal setting, and she is a phenomenal support system (she and my dad). I am positive that all of the things God has blessed me with, is a direct result of my mom's prayers and devotion. I pray that you will also be blessed by this powerful woman of prayer.

Adria McCardy (23)

I Look to You, dear Lord

I look to *You*, dear Lord
I look to the One who sees my children
I look to the One who hears my children
I look to the One who cares about my children
I look to the One who knows my children
I look to the One who feels my children
I look to the One who understands my children
I look to *You*, O God.

I look to *You* for wisdom
I look to *You* for guidance
I look to *You* for insight and knowledge
I look to *You* for courage
I look to *You* for patience
I look to *You* for endurance
I look to *You* for excellence in character
I look to *You*, Awesome Master.

I look to the One who sincerely cares and loves my children
I look to *You*, my Father
I look to *You* to mend their broken pieces
I look to *You* to fill their empty spaces
I look to *You* to cover and protect them
I look to *You* to wrap Your loving arms around them
I look to *You* bless them with *Wisdom*
I look to *You*! I look to *You*! I look to *You*, dear Lord!

- Hope McCardy

Praying For My Children

Precious Father, You have given me four precious jewels to nurture and guide. I must admit that I cannot do the job. Lord, I would not do anything right unless You lead me. Kristi is similar to her dad; Rashad is uniquely himself; Nicole is a mixture of both of us; Adria is like me. How can I know how to meet their needs unless You help me? I realize that they were all made with Your purpose in mind. Help me to mold their characters, but not erase what You have put there. Please give Your daughter guidance. Thank You Lord! In Jesus' name. Amen.

THIS PRAYER WAS taken from my *Little Angels* journal and was written on February 17, 2000. Since this desperate plea to God all those years ago my children have changed, of course, and they continue to change. Those who used to be more like me now seem more like their dad, and then it suddenly flip-flops on us – and sometimes makes a loop. This reality of life has kept me calling out to the Lord on behalf of my children for over twenty-five years.

Going back a couple of decades, one of the most frightening and uncertain times in my life happened about twenty-four years ago when I was pregnant with our third child. It was at this juncture that my husband and I decided that someone should be at home with the children during those early years. I left my relatively secure job as a high school science teacher to take on the challenging role of being a stay-at-home mom. Some told me that I might be making a wrong decision while others praised me for taking such a bold step. Be that as it may, this change was quite scary for me as I had so many questions in my head and only a few answers at that time.

As if that change were not drastic enough, shortly after determining that I would not return to work after the birth of our baby, my husband, Cardinal (Cardy for short), in late September 1991, broke the exciting but unexpected news that his current employer was asking him to relocate. We were being asked to leave the sunny Nassau, Bahamas, to reside in the much colder Philadelphia, Pennsylvania, USA, for a couple of years. So now, not only am I pregnant and leaving my beloved students to stay at home, I have to pack up and deep clean a whole apartment, plan a garage sale, and get sorted out with the necessary documents to live in a new country. On top of that, we now had to consider what to do with our four-year-old preschool daughter, Kristi, and her two-year-old brother, Rashad. Not knowing anything much about the American school system, Cardy came up with a brilliant suggestion.

"Hope," he calmly stated, "You've taught other people's children for the past nine years, why not bring the teaching home and homeschool Kristi and Rashad?"

Easy for him to propose!

My simple retort was, "I can't do that! I have never taught little people before!"

Without even breaking a stride, Cardy replied, "How hard can it be? If you can teach older children, you can surely teach little kids. Hope, you can do this!"

I had no comeback, but I did have a brand new set of apprehensions: a nonpaying job, a new and unfamiliar role, a different country of residence for the next two years, no close family around, and by the way, I'm six months pregnant!

But God! When I tell you that God was my all in all – He was! When I say that I called on Him with all my heart in deep desperation – I did! I sought after my heavenly

Father like a wanderer searching for water in a barren desert. I asked Him for new patience, persistence, and for the ability to teach my children. I pleaded with Him to focus my little ones, to lead and guide them, to place His hand on them, and to make homeschooling agreeable to them. I begged God to give me the compassion to be His servant to my children, to help me see their collective needs, their individual needs, their weaknesses, and their strengths. Every day I had something to seek God for on behalf of my youngsters.

And my Lord did answer – every time! However, it wasn't easy, in fact, many times I felt like giving up, especially when we returned home at the end of 1993, where I faced a fresh challenge and new peer pressure (family and friends) to put the kids in "regular" school. Nevertheless, with my husband's encouragement and God's divine help, we forged ahead, and He (God) allowed me to homeschool them until it was time for each child to go to high school (grade seven).

A Little about God's Faithfulness to My Girls
Like most children, my daughters had issues with sharing stuff at times, the typical power struggles and sibling rivalries, but all in all, they were reasonably easy to teach. They all had strong desires to do well and were hardworking and competitive by nature. Each tried to put forth their best at any sport or extracurricular activity offered to them. They were fairly consistent and diligent and did very well in the

homeschooling system for preschool and grades one to six. Each went on to private high school to receive reports that frequently placed them on the Principal's List or at least the Honor Roll.

Even though it took some time to transition from being homeschooled and settle into regular high school, all three girls coped well and were involved in various clubs and activities including the Student Christian Movement in high school. Before heading off to college, they were all involved in various youth activities at Grace Community Church and became active AWANA leaders and Sunday school teachers.

Kristi, my eldest, has a deep love of music and went from being one of our church's choir members to becoming one of the choir directors. She has also been quite instrumental in rewriting and adapting plays and heading the performances of such. Even in university Kris quickly joined the Gospel Choir and is currently very active in the nursery and events ministries at her new church. She also regularly attends a small group. Kristi is constantly looking for opportunities to grow in her faith by using even her disappointments as springboards to birth new ways to serve the Lord.

My middle daughter, Nicole, has always had a deep love for missions as seen in her commitment to Camp Bahamas. Summer after summer when she was free and available, she spent almost a month at that camp counseling our youth. While in university Nicole also embraced a spring-break opportunity to be part of a one-week missions group to the Spanish-speaking country of Honduras, and then at another time choosing to give up her summer holidays to teach English in South Korea. Needless to say, my poor heart skipped many a beat as she was so far from home. But God was faithful to her, amidst all the lonely, difficult, and challenging times (particularly in South Korea).

As for Adria (my baby), one particular event initiated and carried out by her stands out like no other. Adria has always had a "rescuing heart," and when she was in her last year of high school, she decided to invite her entire graduation class to a social event in our backyard. Adria set out a three-part afternoon and evening consisting of the following:

1. *Fun and games* including basketball, volleyball, swimming, board games, and so on.
2. Two *Breakout Sessions,* entitled *The Next Step,* one for guys and one for girls – where she had a guest speaker for each group.
3. The showing of the movie, *Facing the Giants,* by Alex Kendrick and Stephen Kendrick.

On the morning of the grand event, Adria and I walked through our backyard praying for God's anointing, protection, and special touch on the occasion. It was a cloudy day with a definite warning for rain, so Adria prayed and proclaimed in Jesus' name that it would not rain. We watched in total amazement as the storm clouds dissipated defying the imminent threat of rain.

The whole family joined her in this grand effort and God was faithful to Adria, giving her a delightful and most productive event. Interestingly, a few minutes after the last student left, the rain came pouring down.

GOD'S FAITHFULNESS TO MY SON

Rashad, on the other hand, was another story. He could not focus on anything for more than ten minutes. It was simply a thrill for him to live in daydream land, and I often had to rescue him from the alien planets, which were his favorite places of escape. I had to spend about four times as much time with him than with the girls. He kept me wound up; he kept me busy, and he kept me on my knees. Unlike the girls, he was more interested in just finishing rather than how he finished. I had to sit beside him regularly to get him to do any decent work. Everything seemed a joke to him. I prayed all the time and complained to Cardy many evenings as to what to do. I finally got a significant breakthrough when I discovered that Rashad loved animals, especially dinosaurs, and marine creatures. We capitalized on this knowledge by buying computer software featuring dinosaurs, in particular for the teaching of mathematics, which he loved. We bought dinosaur books, models, learning games – just anything that would capture his interest and keep his attention. He also liked the computer and Nintendo, so whatever I could find to utilize these avenues, we used it to help him. Rashad left me tired and drained most days. But, with God's consistent guidance, much effort, and the one-on-one at home, Rashad did very well in primary school.

Greater challenges came when he entered external high school where no one was going to spend that kind of time with him. As a result of his lack of focus, Rashad missed out on a couple of homework assignments and subsequently re-ceived zeroes for those exercises. He daydreamed and many days had seemingly no real idea of what was done in school that day. Even when I would go to see his teachers and try to explain his special needs to them, they still, understand-ably, found it hard always to have to write the homework on the chalkboard rather than just saying it. You see, because Rashad was not a disruptive child, it was easy for him to go unnoticed. "God, what do I do?" I began reading any litera-ture I could find on all the various symptoms I saw with him. My research suggested that he needed consistent and definite structure. I decided that when Rashad got home from school and could not recall any major points from the subjects he had studied that day…. I made up my mind that I would "revisit" every class that he'd attended and re-teach it from his notes if I had to. This commitment would take hours at times, and then we would begin the day's homework. After a while, he did not like going to school twice a day, and in the tenth grade, he made up his mind to focus in and was able to recall many things he had done on a particular day.

When it came to studying, Rashad would finish studying for an exam in ten minutes, and of course, when tested, he knew very little. I would then have to go and sit with him for hours until he was familiar with what he was supposed to know. I can remember many a time calling out to God and requesting, *Give me another sixty minutes of energy to be with him!* And God was faithful! Sometimes the girls would say, "Mommy, we need you too!" At those times, I would ask Cardy to spend some time with Rashad. Cardy didn't have the kind of patience needed for him and so, before long I was back at it with Rashad, but the little break helped me to finish the task.

Rashad never made the Principal's List, but with a whole lot of work and effort, he did make the Honor Roll quite a few times. And God was faithful. Rashad graduated from high school doing quite well. The whole family was ecstatic and so proud of him.

Shortly after Rashad started college, he felt a calling on his life to go and spend some time on the mission field. And in January 2009, after completing his Associates of Arts Degree, he traveled to Tyler, Texas, to attend the Discipleship Training School at *Youth With A Mission* (YWAM). Rashad completed that training in May 2009. For a part of this training, he spent six weeks in Costa Rica where the YWAM team helped to rebuild homes for the recent earthquake victims there. Rashad continued for an additional five months with the YWAM School of Evangelism and ministered with the group in Oklahoma, Kansas, Illinois, and other places. He was thrilled to be a part of the team.

Now back home in The Bahamas, Rashad's personal experiences have developed in him a heart for helping others. He is currently a tutor in our church's Saturday mornings, Grace Initiative Reading Program, which is a program geared to helping youngsters improve their reading skills. He is also involved in a similar ministry on Tuesday evenings in the AWANA program. You see, as a result of his own unique challenges, God has given him the heart to help others who may struggle. God is faithful!

Homeschooling and external high school are but two areas that I have had to call out to God for on behalf of my children. I have prayed numerous prayers for their health and well-being, attitudes, peer pressure, spiritual attacks, priorities, choices, salvation, tertiary education, their future.... I think you get the picture. So many prayers like the one at the beginning of this section have gone up. Glory, thanksgiving, and praise to Him, as over these many, sometimes challenging and difficult years, I have found God to be so faithful!

My children are all adults now and have all completed undergraduate studies. My three daughters are currently in grad school and working hard. Kristi is set to graduate this spring, even as I am writing this book. My son is working with his dad in the insurance business. He is also continuing in pursuit of his real passion, that of becoming a fantasy fiction writer.

My children all have their various highs and lows, successes and failures, ups and downs. And my job – well, I continue to try to be there for them, to pray for them, and to look to God on their behalf. And my dear sisters, in the midst of all the hard, frightening, and uncertain times, I continue to watch God do great work in their lives – a work that only He can do.

PRAYING GOD'S WISDOM THROUGH THE BOOK OF PROVERBS

WISDOM IS EMPHASIZED over and over again in the book of *Proverbs*. This book teaches us honest truths of how to use wisdom in watching what we say and how we should treat others. It gives us principles for living holy and devout lives that bring honor and glory to God. It uses words like wisdom, knowledge, understanding, and instruction, again and again, to fill our hearts with a perceptiveness and keen alertness as to how to handle any given situation in life. The book of *Proverbs* indeed gives us instructions on how to grow in wisdom.

What an excellent place to get the needed counsel to pray proactively on behalf of our children. Our kids need proper boundaries and limitations in their lives. They have to learn how to relate well to their friends and peers. Someone has to teach them how to deal with difficult people and how to stand up for what is right and not succumb to peer pressure.

And how about the great need for them to be godly and moral, disciplined and determined, insightful and responsible? The answers to all of these wishes and desires for our children, and more, lie in the short six letter word, *wisdom*.

So let's readily accept the gift and privilege to pray for our children. Let's decide right now that we will diligently pray for them to grow in wisdom day by day. I invite you to join me in prayer over the next thirty-one days, guided by a specially selected verse or verses from every chapter of this power-filled book, the book of *Proverbs*. If you miss a day here and there, don't give up, just pick up from where you left off and keep on going. May we as mothers also seek to attain that same wisdom as we pray.

Throughout this prayer book, please take note that you will notice <u>*(names of children)*</u> or the subtitle *Prayer for My Children.* If you only have one child, kindly adapt and read everything in the single voice. Thank you in advance for your patience and understanding.

God's blessings, guidance, strength, and courage go with you as you are also encouraged to adapt the following prayers to the suitable age group of your own children, and don't forget to take the initiative to pray for the future of your offspring as well. Add in your particular situations and be sure to take a few minutes to journal personal insights, comments, or specific breakthroughs. And please remember, we are all on this journey together – no matter how old our respective children are!

Special Note: I am not writing this book as a prayer expert, or as a person who thinks she has all the answers. Quite the contrary, I'm writing as a mother who desperately needs God's wisdom. I am helpless without His guiding hand to show me the right path to follow concerning my children. I am too weak in my own power and need His empowering to stay on that path. Devoid of it, I am sure to fail – every time! It is in this vein that I share these prayers with you.

Blessings and wisdom as only God can give!

DAY 1

THAT THEY LEARN RESPECT FOR THE LORD

Knowledge begins with respect for the LORD.
But those who listen to me will live in safety
and be at peace, without fear of injury.

PROVERBS 1:7A, 33

PRAYER FOR MY CHILDREN

FATHER, YOU KNOW that I love my children, and because of that love I look to You on their behalf. I ask, O Lord, that You would teach <u>(names of children)</u> reverential respect for the Lord, which will also teach them how to respect themselves. Anoint each child with Your wisdom: wisdom that desires to look to You, to search for Your ways. May they truly realize how much You genuinely love and care about them, and even though life's road is often hard, help them to understand that Your heart wants to equip them with the needed knowledge – if they would only look to You. Please teach (names of children) respect for the Lord and the great importance of wisdom. In Jesus' name. Amen.

WORDS OF PROCLAMATION

With God's help and direction (names of children) will grow to respect the Lord more and more every day.

WISDOM NOTES

_____

_____

_____

_____

_____

Day 2

That They Grow in Wisdom and Knowledge

*Wisdom will come into your mind, and
knowledge will be pleasing to you.
Good sense will protect you; understanding
will guard you.
It will keep you from the wicked, from those
whose words are bad.*

Proverbs 2:10-12

PRAYER FOR MY CHILDREN

LOVING LORD, I bring (names of children) before You, and ask that You place a secure hedge of protection around their minds. I pray that they will focus only on the things that are pleasing to You. Please shower my children with Your wisdom, knowledge, and understanding especially in (_____) situation(s) that they are currently going through. Give them a good sense of how to navigate through the various options placed before them. O God, give (names of children) courage to make choices that are within Your will, and may they continue to grow in wisdom, knowledge, and good sense. In Jesus' name. Amen.

WORDS OF PROCLAMATION

May God bless (names of children) with wisdom, knowledge, and good sense.

WISDOM NOTES

_____

_____

_____

_____

_____

Day 3

That They Trust God and not Their Own Understanding

Trust the LORD with all your heart, and don't
depend on your own understanding.
Remember the LORD in all you do, and he will
give you success.
Don't depend on your own wisdom. Respect
the LORD and refuse to do wrong.

Proverbs 3:5-7

Prayer for My Children

THERE IS so much out there to entice my children away from You, precious Lord. Every day, someone or something is pulling at them, *(like _____)*, vying for their attention, seeking to woo them away from Your principles and standards. Teach (names of children) to trust You, to trust in You and not in what they may be seeing or feeling. O Lord, give them eyes and hearts that seek You and desire Your outlook, Your opinion. For it is only You who can provide them with real success. Empower (names of children) and baptize them in Your wisdom so that above all, they would seek to bring honor and glory to God in their everyday choices. Grow them up and mature them spiritually so that they would trust You completely. In Jesus' name. Amen.

WORDS OF PROCLAMATION

May (names of children) hear God's voice clearly and trust Him rather than what they might feel or think.

Wisdom Notes

_____

_____

_____

_____

_____

DAY 4

THAT THEY BE CAREFUL WHAT THEY THINK

Be careful what you think, because your thoughts run your life.

PROVERBS 4:23

PRAYER FOR MY CHILDREN

FATHER, WE KNOW that before we do anything, our actions are dictated by some distinct impression(s) in our minds. Lord, teach (names of children) how to place the needed guards on their thought processes. May they quickly learn not to let careless thoughts meander freely throughout their heads. And Lord, abundantly deposit in each child a spirit of discernment: discernment to be able to discriminate (where possible) what they watch, listen to, where they go, *(list other discriminations)*. O God, please give them the desire and the ability to activate the necessary filters needed to promote healthy and wholesome thoughts about themselves and others. Help my children to choose to think thoughts that would lead to godly lives. In Jesus' name. Amen.

WORDS OF PROCLAMATION

Your grace on <u>(names of children)</u> enables them to choose to think and dwell on healthy and wholesome thoughts that lead to blessed and favored lives.

WISDOM NOTES

_____

_____

_____

_____

_____

DAY 5

THAT THEY WATCH WHAT THEY SAY

*Be careful to use good sense, and watch what
you say.*

PROVERBS 5:2

PRAYER FOR MY CHILDREN

ALMIGHTY FATHER, WE are reminded in Your Word that when we talk too much something sinful is bound to come out of our mouths. Enable (names of children), I pray, to place the needed bridles on their mouths so they can be more conscious and in control of what they say. Establish them in You so that they are well aware of the significant damage careless words can cause, and hence, teach them to monitor seriously the things they choose to speak. Push them to think with conviction about their speech and to make tough decisions, like not talking with haste when they are angry, possibly praying before they open their mouths, *(give more examples)*. O Lord, we know the tongue is quite unruly, so I humbly ask that You would teach my children to watch what they say, and help me to be a good example to them in this most challenging area. In Jesus' name. Amen.

WORDS OF PROCLAMATION

May (names of children) *always be willing to listen and slow to speak.* (That they) *do not become angry easily.* – James 1:19

WISDOM NOTES

_____

_____

_____

_____

_____

DAY 6

THAT THEY DISLIKE WHAT GOD DISLIKES

*There are six things the LORD hates. There are
seven things he cannot stand:
a proud look, a lying tongue, hands that kill
innocent people,
a mind that thinks up evil plans, feet that are
quick to do evil,
a witness who lies, and someone who starts
arguments among families.*

PROVERBS 6:16-19

PRAYER FOR MY CHILDREN

TENDER FATHER, GROWING up can be hard, confusing, challenging, and quite rough for my children, and with the added peer pressure and their raging hormones, it can be all too easy for them to go astray. Reach out to them I pray, and give them Your gentle heart. Enable them to see with Your eyes and to hear with Your ears, so that they can follow You and grow to detest what You detest.

May (names of children) not be prideful, but instead, have humble attitudes. Where they may be prone to telling lies, may they elect in its place, to speak the truth. Teach them to value and protect life, their own and the lives of others. Fill them with Your Word so that their minds would think things that are wholesome and true, and their actions will follow suit. And instead of ridiculous arguments, may they be seekers of Your peace, O Lord. Teach (names of children) to dislike what You dislike. In Jesus' name. Amen.

WORDS OF PROCLAMATION

The God of wisdom is able to lead (names of children) down the right path and do marvelous things in their lives.

Wisdom Notes

_____

_____

_____

_____

_____

DAY 7

THAT THEY GROW IN WISDOM AND UNDERSTANDING

Treat wisdom as a sister, and make under-standing your closest friend.

PROVERBS 7:4

PRAYER FOR MY CHILDREN

WITH SO MUCH going on in the world today that affects my children, gracious Father, all the unhealthy exposure that surrounds them continuously whether in school, on the playground, the media, *(list any other sources)*…be their guide I pray. Amidst it all, give <u>(names of</u>

children) a sincere desire to grow in authentic wisdom: to know how and when to say, "Yes!" and how and when to say, "No!" They need to understand and fully appreciate what is at stake with the choices they make, and what consequences they will ultimately face. There are times when I know it must be so difficult for them to make the right decision(s), because of fleshly desire, peer pressure, the in-thing, and *(give other possible reasons)*.

Father, (names of children) are helpless without Your insight. Lord, please bless my children with a double portion, a triple portion if needed, of Your wisdom and understanding, and may they grow to love pleasing You in all of their choices. In Jesus' name. Amen.

WORDS OF PROCLAMATION
With Your hand on (names of children) shoulders, they will choose to grow in wisdom and understanding every time.

WISDOM NOTES

_____
_____
_____
_____
_____

DAY 8

THAT THEY LISTEN TO WISDOM

Happy are those who listen to me, watching at my door every day, waiting at my open doorway.

PROVERBS 8:34

PRAYER FOR MY CHILDREN

HOLY LORD, THANK You for <u>(names of children)</u> and for the great blessing they are to our family, to others, but especially to me. Lord, my love for them is deep. You know that very well. But I know, that for as much as I love them, that it cannot begin to scratch the surface as to the immense magnitude of Your love for them. Your great love for my children strives to guide their every action and deliver them from any evil loitering in their surroundings – evil seeking to entice them away from Your loving embrace.

Open (names of children) ears to hear Your uncontaminated knowledge, and deposit into their minds and hearts that running after Your wisdom, will ultimately bring the happiness in life that they so desperately seek. Even though the path to insight is often paved with difficult decisions and selfless acts, show my children that it is always in their best interest. Open (names of children) ears to hear Your wisdom, O Lord. In Jesus' name. Amen.

WORDS OF PROCLAMATION

May the song in (names of children) hearts and the tune in their heads ring out, "Hearing God's wisdom and acting on it to bring true happiness...."

WISDOM NOTES

_____

_____

_____

_____

_____

DAY 9

THAT THEY CHOOSE WISDOM

The wise person is rewarded by wisdom.

PROVERBS 9:12A

PRAYER FOR MY CHILDREN

WONDERFUL FATHER, I thank You for the simple, yet profound guidance of Your Word. Still, how is it we just don't often get it? We are so powerfully drawn to our own self-centered and self-focused wants, needs, desires, and frequently so blinded to what is happening around us.

May this not be the case with <u>(names of children)</u>. Educate them continuously as only You can. Open them up to Your truth and anoint them over and over again with a powerful desire to live as unto You. Where they are strong in *(list strengths),* powerfully reinforce these areas and secure them; where they are weak in *(list weaknesses),* strengthen them I pray, and break any bond that seeks to hold them captive. Help <u>(names of children)</u> to get understanding, to get insight, and to choose wisdom in all areas of their lives! Empower my children, today. In Jesus' name. Amen.

WORDS OF PROCLAMATION
It is quite easy and so natural for children to focus on themselves.

May <u>(names of children)</u> choose to be wise and select to focus and depend on God one hundred percent.

WISDOM NOTES

_____

_____

_____

_____

_____

DAY 10

THAT THEY WALK IN LOVE AND UNDERSTANDING

…love forgives all wrongs.
Wise people speak with understanding.
The wise don't tell everything they know.

PROVERBS 10:12-14

PRAYER FOR MY CHILDREN

LOVING FATHER, INSTRUCT <u>(names of children)</u> continuously in the art of loving You, themselves, and others. Your profound example of love to us was beyond all measure. We cannot begin to comprehend how or why You would give up Your One and only Son for us, who are such an ungrateful people. Only You can inspire us to learn that kind of love. Only You can paint (names of children) hearts with Christ's love and care and teach them how to forgive liberally.

While You are showing them how to love, please generously sprinkle their hearts and minds with wisdom and real understanding, so that what they say would be a joy to all who hear. Also, Lord, may they learn to use the necessary tact – knowing when to speak and when to keep quiet. In Jesus' name. Amen.

WORDS OF PROCLAMATION

As God's love administers the gift of grace to all humankind, may (names of children) daily mature in love, discernment, and compassion – becoming generous grace givers.

WISDOM NOTES

_____

_____

_____

_____

_____

DAY 11

THAT THEY DESIRE TO BE GENEROUS AND HELPFUL

Whoever gives to others will get richer; those who help others will themselves be helped.

PROVERBS 11:25

PRAYER FOR MY CHILDREN

LORD, IN AN era when it seems like everyone is fighting for their rights and for what they want, or think they deserve, I ask that You make (names of children) different. Fortify and strengthen them, enabling them to go against the crowd and the masses. I request that You give them generous hearts that desire to help people, to encourage others and lift them up. I pray that You would place them in the company of charitable, wholesome individuals who will strengthen them in this area so that they in turn will give strength. Lead them away from the "me first" self-centered friends who will only pull them down to the greed level. O Lord, where they are weak in being thoughtful and considerate, please nourish and empower them. Bless (names of children) with generous hearts – hearts that are ready to lend a hand. In Jesus' name. Amen.

WORDS OF PROCLAMATION

May (names of children) grasp that whenever they are generous and helpful to others, that somehow and in some way, it always comes back to them – multiplied.

WISDOM NOTES

_____

_____

_____

_____

_____

Day 12

That They Decide Not to be Lazy

Those who work their land will have plenty of food.

Proverbs 12:11a

Prayer for My Children

Father, it is so common today for us to lack diligence and perseverance. It seems like some of us have forgotten the great value and pleasing results of hard work.

May <u>(names of children)</u> never be a part of this group, I entreat. Place in them the desire and tenacity to work hard, for them to seek to accomplish and become all You have planned for them. May nothing be too small or too large for them to pursue industriously. If they are cleaning toilets, raking leaves, scrubbing floors, *(list other tasks)* – may these chores be done to please You. If they are CEOs, doctors, lawyers, *(list specific professions),* push them to perform in their skilled vocations to Your honor and glory. Lord, in whatever (names of children), put their hands to do, may it be done in honesty and integrity, to a level that gets Your approval. Inspire my children to be hardworking, productive individuals I pray. In Jesus' name. Amen.

WORDS OF PROCLAMATION

That (names of children) will learn to see a problem and be determined to work, and to work hard to solve it – to Your honor and glory.

WISDOM NOTES

_____

_____

_____

_____

_____

DAY 13

THAT THEY CHOOSE FRIENDS WISELY

Spend time with the wise and you will become wise.

PROVERBS 13:20A

PRAYER FOR MY CHILDREN

Gracious Father, You let us know that those whom we choose to hang around a lot will eventually have some lasting effect on us. If our friends are edifiers, we will most likely build others up; if they are critical complainers, this too will undoubtedly show up in us.

Anoint (names of children) with a spirit of wisdom and discernment, and encourage them to choose their buddies wisely, I pray. Inspire them from day to day to diligently spend time in Your presence, reading and reflecting on Your Word. Build godly character in my children, and then assist them with their selection of comrades and pals. May they learn to choose close friends who pursue You and want You to be at the center of their lives. May they desire to be a part of healthy Bible studies and small groups, and I ask that You bring them to the place where their greatest aspiration is to get to know You fully, since knowing You is a fundamental prerequisite to choosing wise friends. In Jesus' name. Amen.

WORDS OF PROCLAMATION

As iron sharpens iron, so people can improve each other.
– Proverbs 27:17

WISDOM NOTES

_____

_____

_____

_____

_____

DAY 14

THAT THEY LIVE RESPECTFULLY AND WITH UNDERSTANDING

Respect for the LORD gives life.
Wisdom lives in those with understanding.

PROVERBS 14:27A, 33A

PRAYER FOR MY CHILDREN

FATHER GOD, FEW things bring pure and abundant joy to a mother's soul than to watch her beloved child take his first step, say her first word, hold his bottle by himself, pop her first tooth, or *(give other delightful examples)* – just watching that precious little one grow. Moms have a high respect for the miracle of life created right before their eyes.

In the same way, O Lord, may <u>(names of children)</u> mature to have great respect for You, who is indeed, the authentic life giver. Move them to learn Your ways and to obey Your commands. Open their hearts and minds to know and understand that the same way You breathed life into them at conception, that that same power is available to guide and direct their every step. For who knows better than You every intricate detail about them. Teach my children to respect You, O Lord, and to look to You for the answers to their every question and problem. In Jesus' name. Amen.

WORDS OF PROCLAMATION

May <u>(names of children)</u> learn that the formula for a productive and full life begins with respect for the Lord and then, adding to that, an understanding heart.

Respect for God *plus* an understanding heart *equals* a productive and full life.

WISDOM NOTES

_____

_____

_____

_____

_____

Day 15

That They Seek Good Advice

*Plans fail without good advice, but they
succeed with the advice of many others.*

Proverbs 15:22

Prayer for My Children

Heavenly Father, we recall the story of King Rehoboam when the Israelites requested that he lighten the load that his father, King Solomon, had placed upon them. Rehoboam listened to his people and sought the advice of the wise elders who had served under his father. Though the astute seniors give him excellent advice, he

— 31 —

foolishly rejected it and took in its place the silly advice of his inexperienced young friends.

May this not be the case with (names of children). Stimulate my children to seek good advice from godly and knowledgeable sources, and to avoid (as you would a plague) receiving advice from those who are unfamiliar and lack sense. Give them a strong spirit of discernment to know, with a keen perception, the way in which they should go. As (names of children) face the issues of (state issues) even now, point them to the place where they can receive the best advice. In Jesus' name. Amen.

Words of Proclamation

Let (names of children) see great value in searching for good advice from those gifted to give it, even if it does feel like sandpaper scratching the surface of their skin.

Wisdom Notes

_____

_____

_____

_____

_____

Day 16

That They Depend on the Lord

People may make plans in their minds, but
only the LORD can make them come true.
Depend on the LORD in whatever you do, and
your plans will succeed.

Proverbs 16:1, 3

Prayer for My Children

A LMIGHTY GOD, YOU knew my children even before
they were placed securely in my womb. You knew
every minor and major detail about them. Their unique

personalities were determined masterfully by Your creative hand, and You loved what You fashioned in them.

Encourage (names of children) to look to You. Move them to trust and depend on You. Educate them to know that although they may have a certain direction planned for their lives: in their careers, passions, gifts, talents – that only You can truly give life to their dreams and bring them to fruition. As (names of children) are making plans in *(list areas),* I pray that they will look to You for guidance and direction for every step and that they would make the needed adjustments. Push them to spend ample time with You, freely seeking You for insight, approval, and the know-how, since only You can ensure them success. Teach my children to depend on You. In Jesus' name. Amen.

WORDS OF PROCLAMATION

Impress upon (names of children) hearts and minds, that a decrease in dependence upon themselves and an increase in dependence upon the Lord, will lead to their ultimate success.

Wisdom Notes

_____

_____

_____

_____

_____

Day 17

That They are Always Looking for Wisdom

The person with understanding is always looking for wisdom.

Proverbs 17:24a

Prayer for My Children

Faithful God, the very nature of maturing from children to adults is a continuous pursuit of growing and learning. Wisdom and understanding teach us how to take the most efficient routes to arrive at our various destinations. And we know that we must diligently look to the Holy Spirit for His insight and guidance if we do not want to be perpetually wandering in the desert.

Encourage <u>(names of children)</u> to make it a regular habit of theirs to be continually in the hunt for wisdom. Persuade them to have good judgment concerning their health and welfare, choice of friends, their field of study, boyfriends, girlfriends, husbands, wives, *(list other areas)*. May wisdom be the key that they use to open the door to great and remarkable opportunities – or the key they acquire to lock out harmful intruders and tainted relationships. O Lord, may <u>(names of children)</u> make wisdom their closest and most dearly cherished friend. Bless my children with an abundance of knowledge and understanding, and may they use these practical attributes to their fullest. In Jesus' name. Amen.

WORDS OF PROCLAMATION
When Wisdom calls out, may <u>(names of children)</u> reply, "Yes, I'm here, ready and waiting to receive and welcome your input."

WISDOM NOTES

Day 18

That They Do Right and Run to The Lord for Safety

The LORD is like a strong tower; those who do right can run to him for safety.

PROVERBS 18:10

PRAYER FOR MY CHILDREN

ALMIGHTY GOD, OFTEN when children are young spiritual things can appear to be a drag and old fashion to them. They can't understand why grandma is always singing and talking to the Lord all day, or why in her eyes, God is the answer to every problem.

I pray that (names of children) grow to learn and appreciate that grandma *(or your special person)* was right. Grandma knew that she could run to the Lord for every issue and problem.

May (names of children) decide in their hearts every day to follow in Your footsteps, and where they have veered off the right path, that even today, their hearts would be drawn afresh to You. Likewise, teach my children that You are their heavenly Father – that You want to take care of them. Implant upon their hearts Your great love for them, and may they know that they can run to You for safety, because what is important to them is also important to You. In Jesus' name. Amen.

WORDS OF PROCLAMATION

May (names of children) say to the Lord, *"You are my place of safety and protection. You are my God and I trust you."* – Psalm 91:2

WISDOM NOTES

_____

_____

_____

_____

_____

Day 19

That They Listen to Wise Parenting

Correct your children while there is still hope;
do not let them destroy themselves.
Listen to advice and accept correction, and in
the end you will be wise.

Proverbs 19:18, 20

Prayer for My Children

Loving Father, growing up and maturing can be tough, so very rough on both parent and child. While the child is often adventurous and anxious to try out new things, the parent swerves to the side of playing it safe and seeking to make sure that the child knows both the pros and cons of the desired "adventure."

O Lord, first of all, I ask You for Your great blessing and favor on me as I seek to guide my children. Fill my cup to overflowing with Your wisdom. And then, precious Lord, please move (names of children) to listen to me and their father, as we seek to assist them in making decisions that will have a positive impact on their lives. Inspire us to encourage our children to look to You constantly, to depend on You, to have faith in You. Motivate them daily to read Your Word, to spend time in prayer, and then to apply Your insight and instructions to their everyday lives.

May they grow to appreciate and look forward to the precious knowledge, guidance, rebuke, and correction that You give them directly, or through us. Teach (names of children) to listen to wise parenting and to accept necessary correction. In Jesus' name. Amen.

WORDS OF PROCLAMATION
Children, obey your parents as the Lord wants, because this is the right thing to do. – Ephesians 6:1

WISDOM NOTES

_____

_____

_____

_____

_____

DAY 20

THAT THEY BEHAVE WISELY

Wine and beer make people loud and uncon-
trolled; it is not wise to get drunk on them.
Even children are known by their behavior;
their actions show if they are innocent and good.

PROVERBS 20:1, 11

PRAYER FOR MY CHILDREN

GRACIOUS FATHER, IT is incumbent upon our children
to act wisely: to set limits and boundaries so they can
know how far to go – to be truly aware of when the light
goes from green to amber to red and take heed.

O Lord, bless (names of children) with the wisdom and common sense to put up the needed barriers in their lives that would enable them, in all areas, to display the necessary self-control. Stir in them daily the desire to be in Your presence, soaking up Your Words, Your strength, Your guidance about how they are to live wise and godly lives. May my children be well aware that what they say counts for very little if their actions do not follow suit. Dear Lord, please empower us as parents with the know-how, so that we would be sure to strive to be excellent examples of good behavior to our children, and thus making it almost natural for them to want to behave wisely. In Jesus' name. Amen.

WORDS OF PROCLAMATION

May (names of children) be unequivocally (clearly) aware of the fact that what they say counts for very little if their actions do not parallel their words.

WISDOM NOTES

_____

_____

_____

_____

_____

Day 21

That They Live Right and be Loyal

Whoever tries to live right and be loyal finds
life, success, and honor.
A wise person can defeat a city full of warriors
and tear down the defenses they trust in.

Proverbs 21:21-22

Prayer for My Children

MERCIFUL AND GRACIOUS Father, we live in a world that is constantly changing. What was once right is now wrong, and what was once wrong is now right. How can my children successfully navigate through such ambiguity?

— 45 —

But God, Your ways never change, so I call out to You to successfully navigate (names of children) through an ever-changing society, to Your eternal truth. Demonstrate to them how they are to live right and to be loyal. Teach them to value the things that are of value to You. Anoint them with a God-confidence and show them how to stand firm for what is true. Keep them studying Your Word and spending time with You, anchoring them to Your secure and solid foundation, and fortifying them to live lives of excellence. O Lord, I pray that You would empower (names of children) to live right – to live God-loyal lives. In Jesus' name. Amen.

WORDS OF PROCLAMATION

Right living *plus* loyalty (to God) *equals* a life filled with success *plus* honor. May (names of children) make such a choice every day of their lives.

WISDOM NOTES

_____

_____

_____

_____

_____

DAY 22

THAT THEY BE ASTUTE BUT NOT PROUD

The wise see danger ahead and avoid it.
Respecting the LORD and not being proud will
bring you wealth, honor, and life.

PROVERBS 22:3A-4

PRAYER FOR MY CHILDREN

GUIDING LORD, PLEASE shelter <u>(names of children)</u> in a blanket of Your mighty protection, as there are so many dangerous traps lining the streets on which they travel. When it comes to seeing the danger ahead, may they be farsighted and be able to see clearly, the sketchy objects way ahead of them. And may their reaction not be to drive into the excitement of the apparent danger, but instead, to take the provided detour and avoid the peril altogether.

Bless (names of children) with the spiritual and emotional intelligence of the astute, and fill their hearts with a deep love and respect for You – to love You with everything and in everything. May they grow to realize that it is not all about them, but that it is about their lives seeking to honor and respect You.

Please take away that pride that is more concerned about looking good in man's sight, and replace it with a much deeper love and reverence for You. When it comes to loving You, may they be nearsighted and up close – with eyes fixed on You. May they likewise, be farsighted, seeing You plainly in the distance and knowing that You are everywhere. May (names of children) indeed be sharp, but not vainly proud. In Jesus' name. Amen.

WORDS OF PROCLAMATION
May (names of children) recognize that *pride leads to destruction; a proud attitude brings ruin.* – Proverbs 16:18

WISDOM NOTES

_____

_____

_____

_____

_____

DAY 23

THAT THEY LEARN THE TRUTH AND NEVER REJECT IT

Learn the truth and never reject it. Get wisdom, self-control, and understanding.

PROVERBS 23:23

PRAYER FOR MY CHILDREN

FAITHFUL LORD, MY children are growing up in an ever-changing world where it is becoming progressively harder to decipher the truth from a lie. They are being bombarded daily through the media, the music they listen to, the video games they play, comic books, magazines, billboards, peers, *(list other sources).* They are confronted relentlessly with numerous fallacies and confusing inconsistencies. Only You are equipped to show them the truth.

I look to You, O Lord, to open <u>(names of children)</u> eyes to Your truth. Reveal to them Your real purpose for their lives. Give them a new understanding of what You would like for them to be doing right now: the best kind of friends to hang out with, direction for their future vocation, *(list other desired truth revelations).*

Bless <u>(names of children)</u> with a new and fresh dose of wisdom, understanding, and the precious gift of self-control. For we know that this will enable them to grow and learn Your real purpose and plan for their lives. And may they never reject Your truth. In Jesus' name. Amen.

WORDS OF PROCLAMATION
Guide <u>(names of children)</u> *in your truth, and teach* (them), *my God, my Savior.* — Psalm 25:5a

WISDOM NOTES

_____

_____

_____

_____

_____

Day 24

That They Search after Wisdom and Knowledge

Wise people have great power, and those with knowledge have great strength.

Proverbs 24:5

Prayer for My Children

Loving Father, thank You for <u>(names of children)</u> and for all the gifts and talents You have endowed to them. Thank You for the plan You've determined for each life and each unique personality given. Thank You for Your hand on my children and Your desire for them to achieve to their highest potential.

I sincerely pray for Your continuous anointing of wisdom and knowledge on (names of children), empowering them to be an asset wherever they go, and a positive influence on those around them. May they never use their knowledge vainly or for selfish gain. Instead, give them an eternal outlook on life – seeking to do those things that have everlasting value. Things like sharing with others, taking the time to listen to a friend or neighbor, lending a helping hand, *(list other things)*. May (names of children) grow and mature in their desire to search after wisdom and knowledge. In Jesus' name. Amen.

WORDS OF PROCLAMATION
Though the path to wisdom is laden with steep mountains to climb – when you arrive at the apex, the reward is stronger muscles, greater strength, and a fragrant sense of accomplishment. May (names of children) choose to keep on climbing.

WISDOM NOTES

_____

_____

_____

_____

_____

Day 25

That They Seek to Control Themselves

*Those who do not control themselves are like a
city whose walls are broken down.*

Proverbs 25:28

Prayer for My Children

Heavenly Father, we build walls around cities, office
buildings, homes, monuments, and so on to protect
them. While gates and other security measures are installed
to allow only the right people access, as we seek to protect
the things that we feel are valuable and of high importance.

As (names of children) grow and mature, help them to comprehend their great value, especially to You. May they individually see themselves as a treasure, uniquely formed and fashioned by the Creator, Himself. And Father, where significance has been taken away from them because of having to live in an imperfect world, and with flawed parents, give them a double anointing for any despair suffered. May (names of children) mature to appreciate that personal self-control is the wall constructed around them – protecting the rare ruby, the precious diamond, the child of The King. May my children examine their walls frequently and make the needed repairs to any cracks or leaks discovered. In Jesus' name. Amen.

WORDS OF PROCLAMATION
The Spirit produces the fruit of...self-control. – Galatians 5:22-23

May (names of children) be sure to purchase this prized fruit.

WISDOM NOTES

_____

_____

_____

_____

_____

DAY 26

THAT THEY CEASE LIVING FOOLISHLY

*Giving honor to a foolish person is like tying a
stone in a slingshot.*

PROVERBS 26:8

PRAYER FOR MY CHILDREN

FATHER OF GRACE, we know that a certain amount of
foolishness is inherent in the heart of a child and that it
is our job as parents to help them to see that. However, we
too need Your grace to stomp out our own perpetual foolishness, so that we are adequately equipped to impart wisdom
to our precious children.

Have mercy on us, heavenly Father, and give us the courage and the know-how to discipline our children properly – in love and not in anger. Most of all, I ask and plead loving Father, that You guide (names of children) in the way they should go and teach them how to, first of all, spot a foolish person, and then, how to appropriately respond to that person. And if they are, because of their own insecurity, condoning that silly person in his or her irrational and thoughtless conduct, open their eyes to the folly of this poor response and the intrinsic damage this can cause to both them and the person. May they clearly see that the ultimate message they are relaying is that such bad behavior is acceptable.

Show (names of children) how to walk in Your security and strength, so that they would not ridiculously subject themselves to honoring a foolish person. In Jesus' name. Amen.

Words of Proclamation
Trust the Lord with all your heart, and don't depend on your own understanding. – Proverbs 3:5

May (names of children) learn and follow this verse closely.

WISDOM NOTES

_____

_____

_____

_____

_____

DAY 27

THAT THEY MAKE WISDOM HAPPY

*Be wise, my child, and make me happy. Then
I can respond to any insult.*

PROVERBS 27:11

PRAYER FOR MY CHILDREN

GRACIOUS AND MERCIFUL Father, it takes absolutely no effort to be foolish, no effort to be involved in thoughtless and silly acts, but how arduous the task to follow the path of wisdom. I ask that You baptize <u>(names of children)</u> in pure wisdom – wisdom that comes from Your hand, and give them the passion and the wherewithal to follow it.

Motivate (names of children) to make virtuous choices, with their number one decision being to ask Jesus to be their Lord and Savior. May they also seek to be prudently directed in their everyday decisions: in their selection of friends, with what they decide to watch on television, their reading material collection, and where they choose to go. Guide their hearts especially in picking possible future spouses. Anoint them with wisdom overflowing I pray. *(List other areas where wisdom is needed.)* Encourage (names of children) to grow in wisdom. In Jesus' name. Amen.

WORDS OF PROCLAMATION

May (names of children) comprehend that when Wisdom is contented, they too are happy and greatly satisfied.

WISDOM NOTES

_____

_____

_____

_____

_____

Day 28

That They Elect to Fear the Lord

Those who are always respectful will be happy.

Proverbs 28:14a

Prayer for My Children

Loving Father, there is priceless wisdom in being afraid of certain things, such as touching a stinging jellyfish or putting your hand in an alligator's mouth or walking on hot coals or *(give other examples)*. Then again, Lord, our wisdom is at its highest when we learn to fear You reverentially – to respect and follow You.

Teach (names of children) I pray, to be in awe as to who You are and to learn the righteous fear of God. Push them to respect Your essence and to walk in obedience to Your ways and commands. For when my children are respectful to You, they will transfer this same attitude to their treatment of others – being considerate in what they say and do. Give (names of children) hearts that seek to worship God, I pray. In Jesus' name. Amen.

WORDS OF PROCLAMATION
Since (names of children) love being respected, may they first choose to respect You, and then others.

WISDOM NOTES

_____

_____

_____

_____

_____

DAY 29

THAT THEY RECEIVE CORRECTION

Correct your children, and you will be proud;
they will give you satisfaction.

PROVERBS 29:17

PRAYER FOR MY CHILDREN

GUIDING FATHER, EACH child You have blessed me with is so unique in many ways. Though they may have certain things in common because of a similar heritage, their differences warrant me to deal with each respectively as an individual. I ask that You guide my hand and heart to discipline and correct my children according to their particular temperament, according to what is most operative for the specific child.

Lord, I release my precious gifts of (names of children) to You. Direct me as I seek to instill in them the Fruit of the Spirit. Lead me as I regularly point them to Your Word and its priceless principles. Guide me as I challenge and attempt to dispel any innate foolishness pent up inside my children. Teach me how to set reasonable disciplinary actions for various infractions and to follow through quickly with my word. May their ranting and hurtful words or their shedding of big drops of tears, not cause me to be weakened. Please strengthen Your daughter and move me to be guided by my deep love for them, and my great desire to see them succeed and become all You have created them to be. May (names of children) receive my correction as I seek to follow You. In Jesus' name. Amen.

WORDS OF PROCLAMATION

May (names of children) understand that receiving the needed correction, is a major component in the process of growing in wisdom.

WISDOM NOTES

_____

_____

_____

_____

_____

Day 30

That They Trust in God's Word

Every word of God is true. He guards those
who come to him for safety.

Proverbs 30:5

Prayer for My Children

Loving Father, my children live in a world that wants to make up its own partial truth and challenge the very heart of Your Word. Severe critics surround them, seeking to crush them for even suggesting that Your Word is true. It is becoming progressively harder to live by Your commands, as the world no longer seems to hold them in high esteem.

O Lord, in such a world, cover <u>(names of children)</u> in Your truth I pray, and continually draw them to You.

May <u>(names of children)</u> seek to hide Your precious Word in their hearts and make the decision to live by it. May they find comfort in the fact that when they are targeted for ridicule or negatively labeled, they can run to You for safety and rest. May they recognize and understand that Your Word is consistent – proven over and over again. May my children mature to know that they can trust in Your Word. In Jesus' name. Amen.

WORDS OF PROCLAMATION

Make them ready for your service through your truth; your teaching is truth. – John 17:17

WISDOM NOTES

_____

_____

_____

_____

_____

Day 31

That They Judge Fairly

*Speak up and judge fairly, and defend the
rights of the poor and needy.*

Proverbs 31:9

Prayer for My Children

Gracious and loving Father, give me the wisdom to
be able to teach <u>(names of children)</u> from a very young
age to be fair. Even as they deal with their siblings, friends,
classmates, *(list others),* may they pursue fairness. Show them
how to care about others and not just about themselves.

Father God, I pray that they would grow to recognize the tremendous value of getting good advice. Imprint upon their hearts and minds that such counsel comes from respectable and trustworthy sources, and not necessarily from some charming, likable personality. May they also learn how to make decisions based on sufficient study, adequate knowledge, and most of all, insight and wisdom from You. Enlighten (names of children) so that they would not make hasty decisions based on their fickle feelings. O Lord, empower my children with the ability to judge fairly. In Jesus' name. Amen.

WORDS OF PROCLAMATION

Wrap Your loving arms around (names of children) and teach them to *look to You, dear Lord*, to bless them with *Wisdom*.

WISDOM NOTES

_____

_____

_____

_____

_____

Summary

Loving Father, guide my hand so that it is equipped to teach (names of children) *respect for the Lord,* ensuring that they *grow in wisdom and knowledge* – learning to trust God and not just their own intellectual capacity.

Teach them how to be *careful* in *what they think* and to *watch what they say.*

May they mature spiritually, so that they learn to *dislike what God dislikes,* deliberately pursuing *growth in wisdom and understanding.* Push them to *choose wisdom daily* and to strive to *walk in love* and empathy for others.

Deposit in (names of children) the desire to be generous and helpful – frequently making the decision *not to be lazy.*

When it comes to selecting close buddies, help my children to *choose friends wisely.*

Move and motivate (names of children) to *live respect-fully and with understanding, seeking good advice* and counsel from dependable persons and sources. But most of all, I pray that they will be inspired to *depend on the Lord.*

Stir in my children a deep longing to *always* keep *looking for wisdom* to *do* what's *right, and to* make it their decision to *run* to *the Lord for safety.*

Anoint me, as their mother, with insight and vision in living my own life, so that (names of children) would gladly *listen* to *wise parenting.*

Instill in them intentionality, enabling them to make the calculated choices to *behave wisely,* to *live right, and* to *be loyal* – especially to God.

Please give (names of children) the ability to *be astute but not proud, and may they* select not to brag about their various accomplishments.

Push them to *learn the truth and never* to *reject it,* and may they constantly *search after wisdom and knowledge.*

Help my children to *seek to control themselves,* and may this be an ongoing goal in their lives, which will inevitably fortify them to be able to *cease living foolishly.*

May (names of children) select to *make Wisdom happy* by *electing to fear the Lord* on a day-to-day basis – *receiving His correction* in all that they say and do. I ask You sincerely, to brand upon their hearts the deep faith and knowing that *they can trust in God's Word.*

And may (names of children), formed, shaped, and fortified by You, be greatly empowered to *judge fairly* in all their dealings.

Thank You for Your awesome and mighty hand upon my children, as this enables them to walk, grow, and mature in Your incredible wisdom. In Jesus' name. Amen.

In Closing

CONGRATULATIONS! YOU'VE MADE it to the end of the thirty-one days!

Thank you for joining me in praying for God's wisdom for our precious children. I want to encourage you to look back and see how the Lord, in His grace and mercy, has brought you through this possibly overwhelming, but remarkable time.

You may have to go back and pray specific wisdom prayers for your children time and time again, as certain areas of their lives are harder than others to modify, change, or eradicate altogether. And don't forget to revisit your *Wisdom Notes,* as these may contain God's special personalized messages of encouragement, insight, or instruction to you on their behalf.

Just like us, sisters, our children are a work in progress. Please don't get discouraged if after praying all of these wisdom prayers, they are still a bit lazy and love to sleep, or they are still stubborn and tend to miss the point, or they still can't understand what you are trying to protect them from when you give a caution. Give it time, and let's appreciate that God has ingeniously placed us in their lives, to teach them and to help them decipher between right and wrong. Most of all, let us keep them in prayer, as we are learning these two principles:

1. It is our responsibility to pray and pray and pray some more.
2. It is God's responsibility to answer in His own time and in His own sovereign way. And even when the answer is not to our liking, our trust must be in God and Him alone!

Isn't it indeed a privilege to pray for our children, for them to grow in wisdom, and then watch God answer in ways that only He can?

Didn't we also attain some cherished wisdom along the way? It takes our total dependence on God's wisdom, understanding, and instruction to live our lives in a way that brings Him honor and glory. As we have taken out precious time, this valued time of prayer, focused on praying God's wisdom, knowledge, and understanding for our children – may it be that we also have garnered much for our very own lives!

The attributing selection of verses for this book is but a few of the rare gems taken from the Wisdom book of *Proverbs.* Since the book of *Proverbs* has thirty-one chapters, why not embrace the challenge of reading a chapter a day for the next month, three months, one year, five years, ten years. I believe that you will be sure to find more tasty wisdom nuggets for you and your family in this wisdom-packed book.

You may even choose to take this suggestion to another level. I encouraged you to RPApp (Read, Pray, and Apply):

1. **R** - Read a Proverb a day.
    - Set aside a special time to read and meditate on the chapter – noting the verse or verses that "jump" out at you. You might even choose to journal your verses in a special *Wisdom Journal.*
2. **P** - Pray through the specially selected verse or verses.
    - You may also decide to journal your prayers so that you can record and see how God is working to bless you with ongoing wisdom.

3. **App** - Apply what you have read, meditated on, and covered in prayer.
   - Be determined to apply what God's Word seeks to teach you in living your daily life – particularly in matters of concern relating to your children.
     - For example, if you have been challenged to be *"slow to speak,"* then your particular application might be to choose to *"place a lock on your mouth."* Be quiet! And then intentionally listen to your children with a firm resolve of hearing their hearts properly – before you free up your mouth to speak.

May we all continue to grow and mature in God's gracious and mighty wisdom!

ACKNOWLEDGEMENTS

THANKS TO THE CreateSpace team for your proficiency in setting the text, advice and guidance given, and for providing an appropriate selection for the book cover.

Thanks to the beautiful ladies of my small group: Keleish, Shakia, Rolanda, Jeanine, Letisha, Simone, Kiesha, Faith, and a few friends, Candice, Wendy, and Kayla. Thank you for joining me in praying through these wisdom prayers during our recent *40 Days of Prayer and Consecration*.

Special thanks to Keleish Walkine, who assisted greatly in the final editing process. Thank you for teaching me, working closely with me, helping me through the various steps, and reassuring me when it got tedious.

A heart of love and gratitude to my children: Kristi, Rashad, Nicole, Adria, and my son-in-law, Wendell. Thank you for taking time out to read the prayers and for offering your valued insights and suggestions. I am so indebted to all of you for giving me something to cover in prayer. You make me feel so special in your lives, thank you.

Deep appreciation and love to my supportive husband, Cardinal, who has prayed each and every prayer with me. Thank you for listening to me, encouraging me, for making constructive suggestions in the editing process, and as always, for praying for me and believing in me.

To God be the glory, honor, and praise as any good idea in me, comes directly from Him!

OTHER PRAYER BOOKS BY THE AUTHOR

Be Blessed and Encouraged
31 Days of Praying God's Wisdom for My Husband
31 Days of Praying God's Wisdom for Myself

FOR RELATED DEVOTIONALS, prayer information, interesting articles, poetry, and other exciting stuff, visit us at www.empoweringyourhope.com.

Made in the USA
Middletown, DE
21 November 2018